This book belongs to:

Date:

Website:

Username: Email:

Password:

Security Question 1:

Security Answer 1:

Security Question 2:

Security Answer 2:

Notes:

Website:

Username: Email:

Password:

Security Question 1:

Security Answer 1:

Security Question 2:

Security Answer 2:

Notes:

Website:

Username: Email:

Password:

Security Question 1:

Security Answer 1:

Security Question 2:

Security Answer 2:

Notes:

Website:

Username: Email:

Password:

Security Question 1:

Security Answer 1:

Security Question 2:

Security Answer 2:

Notes:

Website:

Username: Email:

Password:

Security Question 1:

Security Answer 1:

Security Question 2:

Security Answer 2:

Notes:

Website:

Username: Email:

Password:

Security Question 1:

Security Answer 1:

Security Question 2:

Security Answer 2:

Notes:

Website:

Username: Email:

Password:

Security Question 1:

Security Answer 1:

Security Question 2:

Security Answer 2:

Notes:

Website:

Username: Email:

Password:

Security Question 1:

Security Answer 1:

Security Question 2:

Security Answer 2:

Notes:

Website:

Username: Email:

Password:

Security Question 1:

Security Answer 1:

Security Question 2:

Security Answer 2:

Notes:

Website:

Username: Email:

Password:

Security Question 1:

Security Answer 1:

Security Question 2:

Security Answer 2:

Notes:

Website:

Username: Email:

Password:

Security Question 1:

Security Answer 1:

Security Question 2:

Security Answer 2:

Notes:

Website:

Username: Email:

Password:

Security Question 1:

Security Answer 1:

Security Question 2:

Security Answer 2:

Notes:

Website:

Username: Email:

Password:

Security Question 1:

Security Answer 1:

Security Question 2:

Security Answer 2:

Notes:

Website:

Username: Email:

Password:

Security Question 1:

Security Answer 1:

Security Question 2:

Security Answer 2:

Notes:

Website:

Username: Email:

Password:

Security Question 1:

Security Answer 1:

Security Question 2:

Security Answer 2:

Notes:

Website:

Username: Email:

Password:

Security Question 1:

Security Answer 1:

Security Question 2:

Security Answer 2:

Notes:

Website:

Username: Email:

Password:

Security Question 1:

Security Answer 1:

Security Question 2:

Security Answer 2:

Notes:

Website:

Username: Email:

Password:

Security Question 1:

Security Answer 1:

Security Question 2:

Security Answer 2:

Notes:

Website:

Username: Email:

Password:

Security Question 1:

Security Answer 1:

Security Question 2:

Security Answer 2:

Notes:

Website:

Username: Email:

Password:

Security Question 1:

Security Answer 1:

Security Question 2:

Security Answer 2:

Notes:

Website:

Username: Email:

Password:

Security Question 1:

Security Answer 1:

Security Question 2:

Security Answer 2:

Notes:

B

Website:

Username: Email:

Password:

Security Question 1:

Security Answer 1:

Security Question 2:

Security Answer 2:

Notes:

Website:

Username: Email:

Password:

Security Question 1:

Security Answer 1:

Security Question 2:

Security Answer 2:

Notes:

Website:

Username: Email:

Password:

Security Question 1:

Security Answer 1:

Security Question 2:

Security Answer 2:

Notes:

B

Website:

Username: Email:

Password:

Security Question 1:

Security Answer 1:

Security Question 2:

Security Answer 2:

Notes:

Website:

Username: Email:

Password:

Security Question 1:

Security Answer 1:

Security Question 2:

Security Answer 2:

Notes:

Website:

Username: Email:

Password:

Security Question 1:

Security Answer 1:

Security Question 2:

Security Answer 2:

Notes:

B

Website:

Username: Email:

Password:

Security Question 1:

Security Answer 1:

Security Question 2:

Security Answer 2:

Notes:

Website:

Username: Email:

Password:

Security Question 1:

Security Answer 1:

Security Question 2:

Security Answer 2:

Notes:

Website:

Username: Email:

Password:

Security Question 1:

Security Answer 1:

Security Question 2:

Security Answer 2:

Notes:

Website:

Username: Email:

Password:

Security Question 1:

Security Answer 1:

Security Question 2:

Security Answer 2:

Notes:

Website:

Username: Email:

Password:

Security Question 1:

Security Answer 1:

Security Question 2:

Security Answer 2:

Notes:

Website:

Username: Email:

Password:

Security Question 1:

Security Answer 1:

Security Question 2:

Security Answer 2:

Notes:

B

Website:

Username: Email:

Password:

Security Question 1:

Security Answer 1:

Security Question 2:

Security Answer 2:

Notes:

Website:

Username: Email:

Password:

Security Question 1:

Security Answer 1:

Security Question 2:

Security Answer 2:

Notes:

Website:

Username: Email:

Password:

Security Question 1:

Security Answer 1:

Security Question 2:

Security Answer 2:

Notes:

C

Website:

Username: Email:

Password:

Security Question 1:

Security Answer 1:

Security Question 2:

Security Answer 2:

Notes:

Website:

Username: Email:

Password:

Security Question 1:

Security Answer 1:

Security Question 2:

Security Answer 2:

Notes:

Website:

Username: Email:

Password:

Security Question 1:

Security Answer 1:

Security Question 2:

Security Answer 2:

Notes:

Website:

Username: Email:

Password:

Security Question 1:

Security Answer 1:

Security Question 2:

Security Answer 2:

Notes:

Website:

Username: Email:

Password:

Security Question 1:

Security Answer 1:

Security Question 2:

Security Answer 2:

Notes:

Website:

Username: Email:

Password:

Security Question 1:

Security Answer 1:

Security Question 2:

Security Answer 2:

Notes:

Website:

Username: Email:

Password:

Security Question 1:

Security Answer 1:

Security Question 2:

Security Answer 2:

Notes:

Website:

Username: Email:

Password:

Security Question 1:

Security Answer 1:

Security Question 2:

Security Answer 2:

Notes:

Website:

Username: Email:

Password:

Security Question 1:

Security Answer 1:

Security Question 2:

Security Answer 2:

Notes:

Website:

Username: Email:

Password:

Security Question 1:

Security Answer 1:

Security Question 2:

Security Answer 2:

Notes:

Website:

Username: Email:

Password:

Security Question 1:

Security Answer 1:

Security Question 2:

Security Answer 2:

Notes:

Website:

Username: Email:

Password:

Security Question 1:

Security Answer 1:

Security Question 2:

Security Answer 2:

Notes:

Website:

Username: Email:

Password:

Security Question 1:

Security Answer 1:

Security Question 2:

Security Answer 2:

Notes:

Website:

Username: Email:

Password:

Security Question 1:

Security Answer 1:

Security Question 2:

Security Answer 2:

Notes:

Website:

Username: Email:

Password:

Security Question 1:

Security Answer 1:

Security Question 2:

Security Answer 2:

Notes:

Website:

Username: Email:

Password:

Security Question 1:

Security Answer 1:

Security Question 2:

Security Answer 2:

Notes:

Website:

Username: Email:

Password:

Security Question 1:

Security Answer 1:

Security Question 2:

Security Answer 2:

Notes:

Website:

Username: Email:

Password:

Security Question 1:

Security Answer 1:

Security Question 2:

Security Answer 2:

Notes:

Website:

Username: Email:

Password:

Security Question 1:

Security Answer 1:

Security Question 2:

Security Answer 2:

Notes:

Website:

Username: Email:

Password:

Security Question 1:

Security Answer 1:

Security Question 2:

Security Answer 2:

Notes:

Website:

Username: Email:

Password:

Security Question 1:

Security Answer 1:

Security Question 2:

Security Answer 2:

Notes:

Website:

Username: Email:

Password:

Security Question 1:

Security Answer 1:

Security Question 2:

Security Answer 2:

Notes:

Website:

Username: Email:

Password:

Security Question 1:

Security Answer 1:

Security Question 2:

Security Answer 2:

Notes:

Website:

Username: Email:

Password:

Security Question 1:

Security Answer 1:

Security Question 2:

Security Answer 2:

Notes:

Website:

Username: Email:

Password:

Security Question 1:

Security Answer 1:

Security Question 2:

Security Answer 2:

Notes:

Website:

Username: Email:

Password:

Security Question 1:

Security Answer 1:

Security Question 2:

Security Answer 2:

Notes:

Website:

Username: Email:

Password:

Security Question 1:

Security Answer 1:

Security Question 2:

Security Answer 2:

Notes:

Website:

Username: Email:

Password:

Security Question 1:

Security Answer 1:

Security Question 2:

Security Answer 2:

Notes:

Website:

Username: Email:

Password:

Security Question 1:

Security Answer 1:

Security Question 2:

Security Answer 2:

Notes:

Website:

Username: Email:

Password:

Security Question 1:

Security Answer 1:

Security Question 2:

Security Answer 2:

Notes:

Website:

Username: Email:

Password:

Security Question 1:

Security Answer 1:

Security Question 2:

Security Answer 2:

Notes:

Website:

Username: Email:

Password:

Security Question 1:

Security Answer 1:

Security Question 2:

Security Answer 2:

Notes:

Website:

Username: Email:

Password:

Security Question 1:

Security Answer 1:

Security Question 2:

Security Answer 2:

Notes:

Website:

Username: Email:

Password:

Security Question 1:

Security Answer 1:

Security Question 2:

Security Answer 2:

Notes:

Website:

Username: Email:

Password:

Security Question 1:

Security Answer 1:

Security Question 2:

Security Answer 2:

Notes:

Website:

Username: Email:

Password:

Security Question 1:

Security Answer 1:

Security Question 2:

Security Answer 2:

Notes:

Website:

Username: Email:

Password:

Security Question 1:

Security Answer 1:

Security Question 2:

Security Answer 2:

Notes:

Website:

Username: Email:

Password:

Security Question 1:

Security Answer 1:

Security Question 2:

Security Answer 2:

Notes:

Website:

Username: Email:

Password:

Security Question 1:

Security Answer 1:

Security Question 2:

Security Answer 2:

Notes:

Website:

Username: Email:

Password:

Security Question 1:

Security Answer 1:

Security Question 2:

Security Answer 2:

Notes:

Website:

Username: Email:

Password:

Security Question 1:

Security Answer 1:

Security Question 2:

Security Answer 2:

Notes:

Website:

Username: Email:

Password:

Security Question 1:

Security Answer 1:

Security Question 2:

Security Answer 2:

Notes:

Website:

Username: Email:

Password:

Security Question 1:

Security Answer 1:

Security Question 2:

Security Answer 2:

Notes:

Website:

Username: Email:

Password:

Security Question 1:

Security Answer 1:

Security Question 2:

Security Answer 2:

Notes:

Website:

Username: Email:

Password:

Security Question 1:

Security Answer 1:

Security Question 2:

Security Answer 2:

Notes:

Website:

Username: Email:

Password:

Security Question 1:

Security Answer 1:

Security Question 2:

Security Answer 2:

Notes:

Website:

Username: Email:

Password:

Security Question 1:

Security Answer 1:

Security Question 2:

Security Answer 2:

Notes:

Website:

Username: Email:

Password:

Security Question 1:

Security Answer 1:

Security Question 2:

Security Answer 2:

Notes:

Website:

Username: | Email:

Password:

Security Question 1:

Security Answer 1:

Security Question 2:

Security Answer 2:

Notes:

Website:

Username: | Email:

Password:

Security Question 1:

Security Answer 1:

Security Question 2:

Security Answer 2:

Notes:

Website:

Username: | Email:

Password:

Security Question 1:

Security Answer 1:

Security Question 2:

Security Answer 2:

Notes:

Website:

Username: Email:

Password:

Security Question 1:

Security Answer 1:

Security Question 2:

Security Answer 2:

Notes:

Website:

Username: Email:

Password:

Security Question 1:

Security Answer 1:

Security Question 2:

Security Answer 2:

Notes:

Website:

Username: Email:

Password:

Security Question 1:

Security Answer 1:

Security Question 2:

Security Answer 2:

Notes:

Website:

Username: Email:

Password:

Security Question 1:

Security Answer 1:

Security Question 2:

Security Answer 2:

Notes:

Website:

Username: Email:

Password:

Security Question 1:

Security Answer 1:

Security Question 2:

Security Answer 2:

Notes:

Website:

Username: Email:

Password:

Security Question 1:

Security Answer 1:

Security Question 2:

Security Answer 2:

Notes:

Website:

Username: Email:

Password:

Security Question 1:

Security Answer 1:

Security Question 2:

Security Answer 2:

Notes:

Website:

Username: Email:

Password:

Security Question 1:

Security Answer 1:

Security Question 2:

Security Answer 2:

Notes:

Website:

Username: Email:

Password:

Security Question 1:

Security Answer 1:

Security Question 2:

Security Answer 2:

Notes:

Website:

Username: Email:

Password:

Security Question 1:

Security Answer 1:

Security Question 2:

Security Answer 2:

Notes:

Website:

Username: Email:

Password:

Security Question 1:

Security Answer 1:

Security Question 2:

Security Answer 2:

Notes:

Website:

Username: Email:

Password:

Security Question 1:

Security Answer 1:

Security Question 2:

Security Answer 2:

Notes:

F

Website:

Username: Email:

Password:

Security Question 1:

Security Answer 1:

Security Question 2:

Security Answer 2:

Notes:

Website:

Username: Email:

Password:

Security Question 1:

Security Answer 1:

Security Question 2:

Security Answer 2:

Notes:

Website:

Username: Email:

Password:

Security Question 1:

Security Answer 1:

Security Question 2:

Security Answer 2:

Notes:

Website:

Username: Email:

Password:

Security Question 1:

Security Answer 1:

Security Question 2:

Security Answer 2:

Notes:

Website:

Username: Email:

Password:

Security Question 1:

Security Answer 1:

Security Question 2:

Security Answer 2:

Notes:

Website:

Username: Email:

Password:

Security Question 1:

Security Answer 1:

Security Question 2:

Security Answer 2:

Notes:

F

Website:

Username: Email:

Password:

Security Question 1:

Security Answer 1:

Security Question 2:

Security Answer 2:

Notes:

Website:

Username: Email:

Password:

Security Question 1:

Security Answer 1:

Security Question 2:

Security Answer 2:

Notes:

Website:

Username: Email:

Password:

Security Question 1:

Security Answer 1:

Security Question 2:

Security Answer 2:

Notes:

Website:

Username: Email:

Password:

Security Question 1:

Security Answer 1:

Security Question 2:

Security Answer 2:

Notes:

Website:

Username: Email:

Password:

Security Question 1:

Security Answer 1:

Security Question 2:

Security Answer 2:

Notes:

Website:

Username: Email:

Password:

Security Question 1:

Security Answer 1:

Security Question 2:

Security Answer 2:

Notes:

Website:

Username: Email:

Password:

Security Question 1:

Security Answer 1:

Security Question 2:

Security Answer 2:

Notes:

Website:

Username: Email:

Password:

Security Question 1:

Security Answer 1:

Security Question 2:

Security Answer 2:

Notes:

Website:

Username: Email:

Password:

Security Question 1:

Security Answer 1:

Security Question 2:

Security Answer 2:

Notes:

Website:

Username: Email:

Password:

Security Question 1:

Security Answer 1:

Security Question 2:

Security Answer 2:

Notes:

Website:

Username: Email:

Password:

Security Question 1:

Security Answer 1:

Security Question 2:

Security Answer 2:

Notes:

Website:

Username: Email:

Password:

Security Question 1:

Security Answer 1:

Security Question 2:

Security Answer 2:

Notes:

Website:

Username: Email:

Password:

Security Question 1:

Security Answer 1:

Security Question 2:

Security Answer 2:

Notes:

Website:

Username: Email:

Password:

Security Question 1:

Security Answer 1:

Security Question 2:

Security Answer 2:

Notes:

Website:

Username: Email:

Password:

Security Question 1:

Security Answer 1:

Security Question 2:

Security Answer 2:

Notes:

Website:

Username: Email:

Password:

Security Question 1:

Security Answer 1:

Security Question 2:

Security Answer 2:

Notes:

Website:

Username: Email:

Password:

Security Question 1:

Security Answer 1:

Security Question 2:

Security Answer 2:

Notes:

Website:

Username: Email:

Password:

Security Question 1:

Security Answer 1:

Security Question 2:

Security Answer 2:

Notes:

G

Website:

Username: Email:

Password:

Security Question 1:

Security Answer 1:

Security Question 2:

Security Answer 2:

Notes:

Website:

Username: Email:

Password:

Security Question 1:

Security Answer 1:

Security Question 2:

Security Answer 2:

Notes:

Website:

Username: Email:

Password:

Security Question 1:

Security Answer 1:

Security Question 2:

Security Answer 2:

Notes:

Website:

Username: Email:

Password:

Security Question 1:

Security Answer 1:

Security Question 2:

Security Answer 2:

Notes:

Website:

Username: Email:

Password:

Security Question 1:

Security Answer 1:

Security Question 2:

Security Answer 2:

Notes:

Website:

Username: Email:

Password:

Security Question 1:

Security Answer 1:

Security Question 2:

Security Answer 2:

Notes:

Website:

Username: Email:

Password:

Security Question 1:

Security Answer 1:

Security Question 2:

Security Answer 2:

Notes:

Website:

Username: Email:

Password:

Security Question 1:

Security Answer 1:

Security Question 2:

Security Answer 2:

Notes:

Website:

Username: Email:

Password:

Security Question 1:

Security Answer 1:

Security Question 2:

Security Answer 2:

Notes:

Website:

Username: Email:

Password:

Security Question 1:

Security Answer 1:

Security Question 2:

Security Answer 2:

Notes:

Website:

Username: Email:

Password:

Security Question 1:

Security Answer 1:

Security Question 2:

Security Answer 2:

Notes:

Website:

Username: Email:

Password:

Security Question 1:

Security Answer 1:

Security Question 2:

Security Answer 2:

Notes:

Website:

Username: Email:

Password:

Security Question 1:

Security Answer 1:

Security Question 2:

Security Answer 2:

Notes:

Website:

Username: Email:

Password:

Security Question 1:

Security Answer 1:

Security Question 2:

Security Answer 2:

Notes:

Website:

Username: Email:

Password:

Security Question 1:

Security Answer 1:

Security Question 2:

Security Answer 2:

Notes:

Website:

Username: Email:

Password:

Security Question 1:

Security Answer 1:

Security Question 2:

Security Answer 2:

Notes:

Website:

Username: Email:

Password:

Security Question 1:

Security Answer 1:

Security Question 2:

Security Answer 2:

Notes:

Website:

Username: Email:

Password:

Security Question 1:

Security Answer 1:

Security Question 2:

Security Answer 2:

Notes:

Website:

Username: Email:

Password:

Security Question 1:

Security Answer 1:

Security Question 2:

Security Answer 2:

Notes:

Website:

Username: Email:

Password:

Security Question 1:

Security Answer 1:

Security Question 2:

Security Answer 2:

Notes:

Website:

Username: Email:

Password:

Security Question 1:

Security Answer 1:

Security Question 2:

Security Answer 2:

Notes:

Website:

Username: Email:

Password:

Security Question 1:

Security Answer 1:

Security Question 2:

Security Answer 2:

Notes:

Website:

Username: Email:

Password:

Security Question 1:

Security Answer 1:

Security Question 2:

Security Answer 2:

Notes:

Website:

Username: Email:

Password:

Security Question 1:

Security Answer 1:

Security Question 2:

Security Answer 2:

Notes:

Website:

Username: Email:

Password:

Security Question 1:

Security Answer 1:

Security Question 2:

Security Answer 2:

Notes:

Website:

Username: Email:

Password:

Security Question 1:

Security Answer 1:

Security Question 2:

Security Answer 2:

Notes:

Website:

Username: Email:

Password:

Security Question 1:

Security Answer 1:

Security Question 2:

Security Answer 2:

Notes:

Website:

Username:	Email:

Password:

Security Question 1:

Security Answer 1:

Security Question 2:

Security Answer 2:

Notes:

Website:

Username:	Email:

Password:

Security Question 1:

Security Answer 1:

Security Question 2:

Security Answer 2:

Notes:

Website:

Username:	Email:

Password:

Security Question 1:

Security Answer 1:

Security Question 2:

Security Answer 2:

Notes:

Website:

Username: Email:

Password:

Security Question 1:

Security Answer 1:

Security Question 2:

Security Answer 2:

Notes:

Website:

Username: Email:

Password:

Security Question 1:

Security Answer 1:

Security Question 2:

Security Answer 2:

Notes:

Website:

Username: Email:

Password:

Security Question 1:

Security Answer 1:

Security Question 2:

Security Answer 2:

Notes:

Website:

Username: Email:

Password:

Security Question 1:

Security Answer 1:

Security Question 2:

Security Answer 2:

Notes:

Website:

Username: Email:

Password:

Security Question 1:

Security Answer 1:

Security Question 2:

Security Answer 2:

Notes:

Website:

Username: Email:

Password:

Security Question 1:

Security Answer 1:

Security Question 2:

Security Answer 2:

Notes:

Website:

Username: Email:

Password:

Security Question 1:

Security Answer 1:

Security Question 2:

Security Answer 2:

Notes:

Website:

Username: Email:

Password:

Security Question 1:

Security Answer 1:

Security Question 2:

Security Answer 2:

Notes:

Website:

Username: Email:

Password:

Security Question 1:

Security Answer 1:

Security Question 2:

Security Answer 2:

Notes:

Website:

Username: Email:

Password:

Security Question 1:

Security Answer 1:

Security Question 2:

Security Answer 2:

Notes:

Website:

Username: Email:

Password:

Security Question 1:

Security Answer 1:

Security Question 2:

Security Answer 2:

Notes:

Website:

Username: Email:

Password:

Security Question 1:

Security Answer 1:

Security Question 2:

Security Answer 2:

Notes:

Website:

Username: **Email:**

Password:

Security Question 1:

Security Answer 1:

Security Question 2:

Security Answer 2:

Notes:

Website:

Username: **Email:**

Password:

Security Question 1:

Security Answer 1:

Security Question 2:

Security Answer 2:

Notes:

Website:

Username: **Email:**

Password:

Security Question 1:

Security Answer 1:

Security Question 2:

Security Answer 2:

Notes:

Website:

Username: Email:

Password:

Security Question 1:

Security Answer 1:

Security Question 2:

Security Answer 2:

Notes:

Website:

Username: Email:

Password:

Security Question 1:

Security Answer 1:

Security Question 2:

Security Answer 2:

Notes:

Website:

Username: Email:

Password:

Security Question 1:

Security Answer 1:

Security Question 2:

Security Answer 2:

Notes:

Website:

Username: Email:

Password:

Security Question 1:

Security Answer 1:

Security Question 2:

Security Answer 2:

Notes:

Website:

Username: Email:

Password:

Security Question 1:

Security Answer 1:

Security Question 2:

Security Answer 2:

Notes:

Website:

Username: Email:

Password:

Security Question 1:

Security Answer 1:

Security Question 2:

Security Answer 2:

Notes:

Website:

Username: Email:

Password:

Security Question 1:

Security Answer 1:

Security Question 2:

Security Answer 2:

Notes:

Website:

Username: Email:

Password:

Security Question 1:

Security Answer 1:

Security Question 2:

Security Answer 2:

Notes:

Website:

Username: Email:

Password:

Security Question 1:

Security Answer 1:

Security Question 2:

Security Answer 2:

Notes:

Website:

Username: Email:

Password:

Security Question 1:

Security Answer 1:

Security Question 2:

Security Answer 2:

Notes:

Website:

Username: Email:

Password:

Security Question 1:

Security Answer 1:

Security Question 2:

Security Answer 2:

Notes:

Website:

Username: Email:

Password:

Security Question 1:

Security Answer 1:

Security Question 2:

Security Answer 2:

Notes:

Website:

Username: Email:

Password:

Security Question 1:

Security Answer 1:

Security Question 2:

Security Answer 2:

Notes:

Website:

Username: Email:

Password:

Security Question 1:

Security Answer 1:

Security Question 2:

Security Answer 2:

Notes:

Website:

Username: Email:

Password:

Security Question 1:

Security Answer 1:

Security Question 2:

Security Answer 2:

Notes:

Website:

Username: Email:

Password:

Security Question 1:

Security Answer 1:

Security Question 2:

Security Answer 2:

Notes:

Website:

Username: Email:

Password:

Security Question 1:

Security Answer 1:

Security Question 2:

Security Answer 2:

Notes:

Website:

Username: Email:

Password:

Security Question 1:

Security Answer 1:

Security Question 2:

Security Answer 2:

Notes:

Website:

Username:　　　　Email:

Password:

Security Question 1:

Security Answer 1:

Security Question 2:

Security Answer 2:

Notes:

Website:

Username:　　　　Email:

Password:

Security Question 1:

Security Answer 1:

Security Question 2:

Security Answer 2:

Notes:

Website:

Username:　　　　Email:

Password:

Security Question 1:

Security Answer 1:

Security Question 2:

Security Answer 2:

Notes:

Website:

Username: Email:

Password:

Security Question 1:

Security Answer 1:

Security Question 2:

Security Answer 2:

Notes:

Website:

Username: Email:

Password:

Security Question 1:

Security Answer 1:

Security Question 2:

Security Answer 2:

Notes:

Website:

Username: Email:

Password:

Security Question 1:

Security Answer 1:

Security Question 2:

Security Answer 2:

Notes:

Website:

Username: Email:

Password:

Security Question 1:

Security Answer 1:

Security Question 2:

Security Answer 2:

Notes:

Website:

Username: Email:

Password:

Security Question 1:

Security Answer 1:

Security Question 2:

Security Answer 2:

Notes:

Website:

Username: Email:

Password:

Security Question 1:

Security Answer 1:

Security Question 2:

Security Answer 2:

Notes:

Website:

Username: Email:

Password:

Security Question 1:

Security Answer 1:

Security Question 2:

Security Answer 2:

Notes:

Website:

Username: Email:

Password:

Security Question 1:

Security Answer 1:

Security Question 2:

Security Answer 2:

Notes:

Website:

Username: Email:

Password:

Security Question 1:

Security Answer 1:

Security Question 2:

Security Answer 2:

Notes:

Website:

Username: Email:

Password:

Security Question 1:

Security Answer 1:

Security Question 2:

Security Answer 2:

Notes:

Website:

Username: Email:

Password:

Security Question 1:

Security Answer 1:

Security Question 2:

Security Answer 2:

Notes:

Website:

Username: Email:

Password:

Security Question 1:

Security Answer 1:

Security Question 2:

Security Answer 2:

Notes:

L

Website:

Username: Email:

Password:

Security Question 1:

Security Answer 1:

Security Question 2:

Security Answer 2:

Notes:

Website:

Username: Email:

Password:

Security Question 1:

Security Answer 1:

Security Question 2:

Security Answer 2:

Notes:

Website:

Username: Email:

Password:

Security Question 1:

Security Answer 1:

Security Question 2:

Security Answer 2:

Notes:

Website:

Username: Email:

Password:

Security Question 1:

Security Answer 1:

Security Question 2:

Security Answer 2:

Notes:

Website:

Username: Email:

Password:

Security Question 1:

Security Answer 1:

Security Question 2:

Security Answer 2:

Notes:

Website:

Username: Email:

Password:

Security Question 1:

Security Answer 1:

Security Question 2:

Security Answer 2:

Notes:

L

Website:

Username: Email:

Password:

Security Question 1:

Security Answer 1:

Security Question 2:

Security Answer 2:

Notes:

Website:

Username: Email:

Password:

Security Question 1:

Security Answer 1:

Security Question 2:

Security Answer 2:

Notes:

Website:

Username: Email:

Password:

Security Question 1:

Security Answer 1:

Security Question 2:

Security Answer 2:

Notes:

Website:

Username: Email:

Password:

Security Question 1:

Security Answer 1:

Security Question 2:

Security Answer 2:

Notes:

Website:

Username: Email:

Password:

Security Question 1:

Security Answer 1:

Security Question 2:

Security Answer 2:

Notes:

Website:

Username: Email:

Password:

Security Question 1:

Security Answer 1:

Security Question 2:

Security Answer 2:

Notes:

Website:

Username: Email:

Password:

Security Question 1:

Security Answer 1:

Security Question 2:

Security Answer 2:

Notes:

Website:

Username: Email:

Password:

Security Question 1:

Security Answer 1:

Security Question 2:

Security Answer 2:

Notes:

Website:

Username: Email:

Password:

Security Question 1:

Security Answer 1:

Security Question 2:

Security Answer 2:

Notes:

Website:

Username: Email:

Password:

Security Question 1:

Security Answer 1:

Security Question 2:

Security Answer 2:

Notes:

Website:

Username: Email:

Password:

Security Question 1:

Security Answer 1:

Security Question 2:

Security Answer 2:

Notes:

Website:

Username: Email:

Password:

Security Question 1:

Security Answer 1:

Security Question 2:

Security Answer 2:

Notes:

Website:

Username: Email:

Password:

Security Question 1:

Security Answer 1:

Security Question 2:

Security Answer 2:

Notes:

Website:

Username: Email:

Password:

Security Question 1:

Security Answer 1:

Security Question 2:

Security Answer 2:

Notes:

Website:

Username: Email:

Password:

Security Question 1:

Security Answer 1:

Security Question 2:

Security Answer 2:

Notes:

Website:

Username: Email:

Password:

Security Question 1:

Security Answer 1:

Security Question 2:

Security Answer 2:

Notes:

Website:

Username: Email:

Password:

Security Question 1:

Security Answer 1:

Security Question 2:

Security Answer 2:

Notes:

Website:

Username: Email:

Password:

Security Question 1:

Security Answer 1:

Security Question 2:

Security Answer 2:

Notes:

Website:

Username: Email:

Password:

Security Question 1:

Security Answer 1:

Security Question 2:

Security Answer 2:

Notes:

Website:

Username: Email:

Password:

Security Question 1:

Security Answer 1:

Security Question 2:

Security Answer 2:

Notes:

Website:

Username: Email:

Password:

Security Question 1:

Security Answer 1:

Security Question 2:

Security Answer 2:

Notes:

Website:

Username: Email:

Password:

Security Question 1:

Security Answer 1:

Security Question 2:

Security Answer 2:

Notes:

Website:

Username: Email:

Password:

Security Question 1:

Security Answer 1:

Security Question 2:

Security Answer 2:

Notes:

Website:

Username: Email:

Password:

Security Question 1:

Security Answer 1:

Security Question 2:

Security Answer 2:

Notes:

Website:

Username: Email:

Password:

Security Question 1:

Security Answer 1:

Security Question 2:

Security Answer 2:

Notes:

Website:

Username: Email:

Password:

Security Question 1:

Security Answer 1:

Security Question 2:

Security Answer 2:

Notes:

Website:

Username: Email:

Password:

Security Question 1:

Security Answer 1:

Security Question 2:

Security Answer 2:

Notes:

Website:

Username: Email:

Password:

Security Question 1:

Security Answer 1:

Security Question 2:

Security Answer 2:

Notes:

Website:

Username: Email:

Password:

Security Question 1:

Security Answer 1:

Security Question 2:

Security Answer 2:

Notes:

Website:

Username: Email:

Password:

Security Question 1:

Security Answer 1:

Security Question 2:

Security Answer 2:

Notes:

Website:

Username: Email:

Password:

Security Question 1:

Security Answer 1:

Security Question 2:

Security Answer 2:

Notes:

Website:

Username: Email:

Password:

Security Question 1:

Security Answer 1:

Security Question 2:

Security Answer 2:

Notes:

Website:

Username: Email:

Password:

Security Question 1:

Security Answer 1:

Security Question 2:

Security Answer 2:

Notes:

Website:

Username: Email:

Password:

Security Question 1:

Security Answer 1:

Security Question 2:

Security Answer 2:

Notes:

Website:

Username: Email:

Password:

Security Question 1:

Security Answer 1:

Security Question 2:

Security Answer 2:

Notes:

Website:

Username: Email:

Password:

Security Question 1:

Security Answer 1:

Security Question 2:

Security Answer 2:

Notes:

Website:

Username: | Email:

Password:

Security Question 1:

Security Answer 1:

Security Question 2:

Security Answer 2:

Notes:

Website:

Username: | Email:

Password:

Security Question 1:

Security Answer 1:

Security Question 2:

Security Answer 2:

Notes:

Website:

Username: | Email:

Password:

Security Question 1:

Security Answer 1:

Security Question 2:

Security Answer 2:

Notes:

Website:

Username: Email:

Password:

Security Question 1:

Security Answer 1:

Security Question 2:

Security Answer 2:

Notes:

Website:

Username: Email:

Password:

Security Question 1:

Security Answer 1:

Security Question 2:

Security Answer 2:

Notes:

Website:

Username: Email:

Password:

Security Question 1:

Security Answer 1:

Security Question 2:

Security Answer 2:

Notes:

N

Website:

Username: Email:

Password:

Security Question 1:

Security Answer 1:

Security Question 2:

Security Answer 2:

Notes:

Website:

Username: Email:

Password:

Security Question 1:

Security Answer 1:

Security Question 2:

Security Answer 2:

Notes:

Website:

Username: Email:

Password:

Security Question 1:

Security Answer 1:

Security Question 2:

Security Answer 2:

Notes:

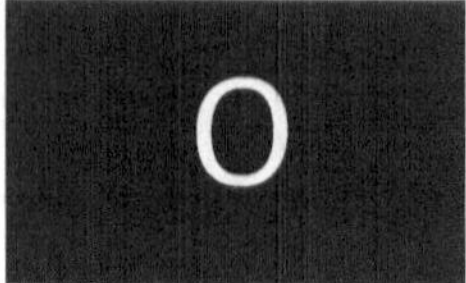

Website:

Username: Email:

Password:

Security Question 1:

Security Answer 1:

Security Question 2:

Security Answer 2:

Notes:

Website:

Username: Email:

Password:

Security Question 1:

Security Answer 1:

Security Question 2:

Security Answer 2:

Notes:

Website:

Username: Email:

Password:

Security Question 1:

Security Answer 1:

Security Question 2:

Security Answer 2:

Notes:

Website:

Username: Email:

Password:

Security Question 1:

Security Answer 1:

Security Question 2:

Security Answer 2:

Notes:

Website:

Username: Email:

Password:

Security Question 1:

Security Answer 1:

Security Question 2:

Security Answer 2:

Notes:

Website:

Username: Email:

Password:

Security Question 1:

Security Answer 1:

Security Question 2:

Security Answer 2:

Notes:

Website:

Username: Email:

Password:

Security Question 1:

Security Answer 1:

Security Question 2:

Security Answer 2:

Notes:

Website:

Username: Email:

Password:

Security Question 1:

Security Answer 1:

Security Question 2:

Security Answer 2:

Notes:

Website:

Username: Email:

Password:

Security Question 1:

Security Answer 1:

Security Question 2:

Security Answer 2:

Notes:

Website:

Username: Email:

Password:

Security Question 1:

Security Answer 1:

Security Question 2:

Security Answer 2:

Notes:

Website:

Username: Email:

Password:

Security Question 1:

Security Answer 1:

Security Question 2:

Security Answer 2:

Notes:

Website:

Username: Email:

Password:

Security Question 1:

Security Answer 1:

Security Question 2:

Security Answer 2:

Notes:

Website:

Username: Email:

Password:

Security Question 1:

Security Answer 1:

Security Question 2:

Security Answer 2:

Notes:

Website:

Username: Email:

Password:

Security Question 1:

Security Answer 1:

Security Question 2:

Security Answer 2:

Notes:

Website:

Username: Email:

Password:

Security Question 1:

Security Answer 1:

Security Question 2:

Security Answer 2:

Notes:

Website:

Username: Email:

Password:

Security Question 1:

Security Answer 1:

Security Question 2:

Security Answer 2:

Notes:

Website:

Username: Email:

Password:

Security Question 1:

Security Answer 1:

Security Question 2:

Security Answer 2:

Notes:

Website:

Username: Email:

Password:

Security Question 1:

Security Answer 1:

Security Question 2:

Security Answer 2:

Notes:

Website:

Username: Email:

Password:

Security Question 1:

Security Answer 1:

Security Question 2:

Security Answer 2:

Notes:

Website:

Username: Email:

Password:

Security Question 1:

Security Answer 1:

Security Question 2:

Security Answer 2:

Notes:

Website:

Username: Email:

Password:

Security Question 1:

Security Answer 1:

Security Question 2:

Security Answer 2:

Notes:

P

Website:

Username: Email:

Password:

Security Question 1:

Security Answer 1:

Security Question 2:

Security Answer 2:

Notes:

Website:

Username: Email:

Password:

Security Question 1:

Security Answer 1:

Security Question 2:

Security Answer 2:

Notes:

Website:

Username: Email:

Password:

Security Question 1:

Security Answer 1:

Security Question 2:

Security Answer 2:

Notes:

Website:

Username: Email:

Password:

Security Question 1:

Security Answer 1:

Security Question 2:

Security Answer 2:

Notes:

Website:

Username: Email:

Password:

Security Question 1:

Security Answer 1:

Security Question 2:

Security Answer 2:

Notes:

Website:

Username: Email:

Password:

Security Question 1:

Security Answer 1:

Security Question 2:

Security Answer 2:

Notes:

P

Website:

Username: Email:

Password:

Security Question 1:

Security Answer 1:

Security Question 2:

Security Answer 2:

Notes:

Website:

Username: Email:

Password:

Security Question 1:

Security Answer 1:

Security Question 2:

Security Answer 2:

Notes:

Website:

Username: Email:

Password:

Security Question 1:

Security Answer 1:

Security Question 2:

Security Answer 2:

Notes:

Website:

Username: | Email:

Password:

Security Question 1:

Security Answer 1:

Security Question 2:

Security Answer 2:

Notes:

Website:

Username: | Email:

Password:

Security Question 1:

Security Answer 1:

Security Question 2:

Security Answer 2:

Notes:

Website:

Username: | Email:

Password:

Security Question 1:

Security Answer 1:

Security Question 2:

Security Answer 2:

Notes:

Website:

Username: Email:

Password:

Security Question 1:

Security Answer 1:

Security Question 2:

Security Answer 2:

Notes:

Website:

Username: Email:

Password:

Security Question 1:

Security Answer 1:

Security Question 2:

Security Answer 2:

Notes:

Website:

Username: Email:

Password:

Security Question 1:

Security Answer 1:

Security Question 2:

Security Answer 2:

Notes:

Website:

Username: Email:

Password:

Security Question 1:

Security Answer 1:

Security Question 2:

Security Answer 2:

Notes:

Website:

Username: Email:

Password:

Security Question 1:

Security Answer 1:

Security Question 2:

Security Answer 2:

Notes:

Website:

Username: Email:

Password:

Security Question 1:

Security Answer 1:

Security Question 2:

Security Answer 2:

Notes:

Q

Website:

Username: Email:

Password:

Security Question 1:

Security Answer 1:

Security Question 2:

Security Answer 2:

Notes:

Website:

Username: Email:

Password:

Security Question 1:

Security Answer 1:

Security Question 2:

Security Answer 2:

Notes:

Website:

Username: Email:

Password:

Security Question 1:

Security Answer 1:

Security Question 2:

Security Answer 2:

Notes:

Q

Website:

Username: ____________________ Email: ____________________

Password:

Security Question 1:

Security Answer 1:

Security Question 2:

Security Answer 2:

Notes:

Website:

Username: ____________________ Email: ____________________

Password:

Security Question 1:

Security Answer 1:

Security Question 2:

Security Answer 2:

Notes:

Website:

Username: ____________________ Email: ____________________

Password:

Security Question 1:

Security Answer 1:

Security Question 2:

Security Answer 2:

Notes:

Q

Website:

Username: Email:

Password:

Security Question 1:

Security Answer 1:

Security Question 2:

Security Answer 2:

Notes:

Website:

Username: Email:

Password:

Security Question 1:

Security Answer 1:

Security Question 2:

Security Answer 2:

Notes:

Website:

Username: Email:

Password:

Security Question 1:

Security Answer 1:

Security Question 2:

Security Answer 2:

Notes:

Website:

Username: Email:

Password:

Security Question 1:

Security Answer 1:

Security Question 2:

Security Answer 2:

Notes:

Website:

Username: Email:

Password:

Security Question 1:

Security Answer 1:

Security Question 2:

Security Answer 2:

Notes:

Website:

Username: Email:

Password:

Security Question 1:

Security Answer 1:

Security Question 2:

Security Answer 2:

Notes:

Q

Website:

Username: Email:

Password:

Security Question 1:

Security Answer 1:

Security Question 2:

Security Answer 2:

Notes:

Website:

Username: Email:

Password:

Security Question 1:

Security Answer 1:

Security Question 2:

Security Answer 2:

Notes:

Website:

Username: Email:

Password:

Security Question 1:

Security Answer 1:

Security Question 2:

Security Answer 2:

Notes:

Website:

Username: Email:

Password:

Security Question 1:

Security Answer 1:

Security Question 2:

Security Answer 2:

Notes:

Website:

Username: Email:

Password:

Security Question 1:

Security Answer 1:

Security Question 2:

Security Answer 2:

Notes:

Website:

Username: Email:

Password:

Security Question 1:

Security Answer 1:

Security Question 2:

Security Answer 2:

Notes:

R

Website:

Username: Email:

Password:

Security Question 1:

Security Answer 1:

Security Question 2:

Security Answer 2:

Notes:

Website:

Username: Email:

Password:

Security Question 1:

Security Answer 1:

Security Question 2:

Security Answer 2:

Notes:

Website:

Username: Email:

Password:

Security Question 1:

Security Answer 1:

Security Question 2:

Security Answer 2:

Notes:

Website:

Username: Email:

Password:

Security Question 1:

Security Answer 1:

Security Question 2:

Security Answer 2:

Notes:

Website:

Username: Email:

Password:

Security Question 1:

Security Answer 1:

Security Question 2:

Security Answer 2:

Notes:

Website:

Username: Email:

Password:

Security Question 1:

Security Answer 1:

Security Question 2:

Security Answer 2:

Notes:

Website:

Username: Email:

Password:

Security Question 1:

Security Answer 1:

Security Question 2:

Security Answer 2:

Notes:

Website:

Username: Email:

Password:

Security Question 1:

Security Answer 1:

Security Question 2:

Security Answer 2:

Notes:

Website:

Username: Email:

Password:

Security Question 1:

Security Answer 1:

Security Question 2:

Security Answer 2:

Notes:

Website:

Username: Email:

Password:

Security Question 1:

Security Answer 1:

Security Question 2:

Security Answer 2:

Notes:

Website:

Username: Email:

Password:

Security Question 1:

Security Answer 1:

Security Question 2:

Security Answer 2:

Notes:

Website:

Username: Email:

Password:

Security Question 1:

Security Answer 1:

Security Question 2:

Security Answer 2:

Notes:

Website:

Username: ___________________ Email: ___________________

Password:

Security Question 1:

Security Answer 1:

Security Question 2:

Security Answer 2:

Notes:

Website:

Username: ___________________ Email: ___________________

Password:

Security Question 1:

Security Answer 1:

Security Question 2:

Security Answer 2:

Notes:

Website:

Username: ___________________ Email: ___________________

Password:

Security Question 1:

Security Answer 1:

Security Question 2:

Security Answer 2:

Notes:

Website:

Username: Email:

Password:

Security Question 1:

Security Answer 1:

Security Question 2:

Security Answer 2:

Notes:

Website:

Username: Email:

Password:

Security Question 1:

Security Answer 1:

Security Question 2:

Security Answer 2:

Notes:

Website:

Username: Email:

Password:

Security Question 1:

Security Answer 1:

Security Question 2:

Security Answer 2:

Notes:

S

Website:

Username: | Email:

Password:

Security Question 1:

Security Answer 1:

Security Question 2:

Security Answer 2:

Notes:

Website:

Username: | Email:

Password:

Security Question 1:

Security Answer 1:

Security Question 2:

Security Answer 2:

Notes:

Website:

Username: | Email:

Password:

Security Question 1:

Security Answer 1:

Security Question 2:

Security Answer 2:

Notes:

Website:

Username: Email:

Password:

Security Question 1:

Security Answer 1:

Security Question 2:

Security Answer 2:

Notes:

Website:

Username: Email:

Password:

Security Question 1:

Security Answer 1:

Security Question 2:

Security Answer 2:

Notes:

Website:

Username: Email:

Password:

Security Question 1:

Security Answer 1:

Security Question 2:

Security Answer 2:

Notes:

S

Website:

Username: Email:

Password:

Security Question 1:

Security Answer 1:

Security Question 2:

Security Answer 2:

Notes:

Website:

Username: Email:

Password:

Security Question 1:

Security Answer 1:

Security Question 2:

Security Answer 2:

Notes:

Website:

Username: Email:

Password:

Security Question 1:

Security Answer 1:

Security Question 2:

Security Answer 2:

Notes:

S

Website:

Username: Email:

Password:

Security Question 1:

Security Answer 1:

Security Question 2:

Security Answer 2:

Notes:

Website:

Username: Email:

Password:

Security Question 1:

Security Answer 1:

Security Question 2:

Security Answer 2:

Notes:

Website:

Username: Email:

Password:

Security Question 1:

Security Answer 1:

Security Question 2:

Security Answer 2:

Notes:

S

Website:

Username: Email:

Password:

Security Question 1:

Security Answer 1:

Security Question 2:

Security Answer 2:

Notes:

Website:

Username: Email:

Password:

Security Question 1:

Security Answer 1:

Security Question 2:

Security Answer 2:

Notes:

Website:

Username: Email:

Password:

Security Question 1:

Security Answer 1:

Security Question 2:

Security Answer 2:

Notes:

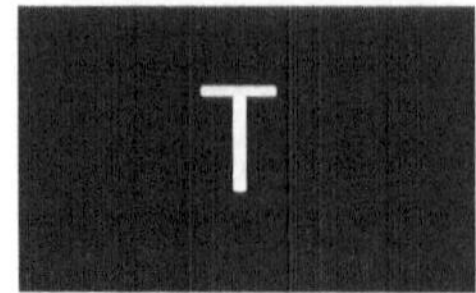

Website:

Username: Email:

Password:

Security Question 1:

Security Answer 1:

Security Question 2:

Security Answer 2:

Notes:

Website:

Username: Email:

Password:

Security Question 1:

Security Answer 1:

Security Question 2:

Security Answer 2:

Notes:

Website:

Username: Email:

Password:

Security Question 1:

Security Answer 1:

Security Question 2:

Security Answer 2:

Notes:

T

Website:

Username: **Email:**

Password:

Security Question 1:

Security Answer 1:

Security Question 2:

Security Answer 2:

Notes:

Website:

Username: **Email:**

Password:

Security Question 1:

Security Answer 1:

Security Question 2:

Security Answer 2:

Notes:

Website:

Username: **Email:**

Password:

Security Question 1:

Security Answer 1:

Security Question 2:

Security Answer 2:

Notes:

Website:

Username: Email:

Password:

Security Question 1:

Security Answer 1:

Security Question 2:

Security Answer 2:

Notes:

Website:

Username: Email:

Password:

Security Question 1:

Security Answer 1:

Security Question 2:

Security Answer 2:

Notes:

Website:

Username: Email:

Password:

Security Question 1:

Security Answer 1:

Security Question 2:

Security Answer 2:

Notes:

T

Website:

Username: Email:

Password:

Security Question 1:

Security Answer 1:

Security Question 2:

Security Answer 2:

Notes:

Website:

Username: Email:

Password:

Security Question 1:

Security Answer 1:

Security Question 2:

Security Answer 2:

Notes:

Website:

Username: Email:

Password:

Security Question 1:

Security Answer 1:

Security Question 2:

Security Answer 2:

Notes:

Website:

Username: | Email:

Password:

Security Question 1:

Security Answer 1:

Security Question 2:

Security Answer 2:

Notes:

Website:

Username: | Email:

Password:

Security Question 1:

Security Answer 1:

Security Question 2:

Security Answer 2:

Notes:

Website:

Username: | Email:

Password:

Security Question 1:

Security Answer 1:

Security Question 2:

Security Answer 2:

Notes:

Website:

Username: Email:

Password:

Security Question 1:

Security Answer 1:

Security Question 2:

Security Answer 2:

Notes:

Website:

Username: Email:

Password:

Security Question 1:

Security Answer 1:

Security Question 2:

Security Answer 2:

Notes:

Website:

Username: Email:

Password:

Security Question 1:

Security Answer 1:

Security Question 2:

Security Answer 2:

Notes:

Website:

Username: Email:

Password:

Security Question 1:

Security Answer 1:

Security Question 2:

Security Answer 2:

Notes:

Website:

Username: Email:

Password:

Security Question 1:

Security Answer 1:

Security Question 2:

Security Answer 2:

Notes:

Website:

Username: Email:

Password:

Security Question 1:

Security Answer 1:

Security Question 2:

Security Answer 2:

Notes:

Website:

Username: Email:

Password:

Security Question 1:

Security Answer 1:

Security Question 2:

Security Answer 2:

Notes:

Website:

Username: Email:

Password:

Security Question 1:

Security Answer 1:

Security Question 2:

Security Answer 2:

Notes:

Website:

Username: Email:

Password:

Security Question 1:

Security Answer 1:

Security Question 2:

Security Answer 2:

Notes:

U

Website:

Username:	Email:

Password:

Security Question 1:

Security Answer 1:

Security Question 2:

Security Answer 2:

Notes:

Website:

Username:	Email:

Password:

Security Question 1:

Security Answer 1:

Security Question 2:

Security Answer 2:

Notes:

Website:

Username:	Email:

Password:

Security Question 1:

Security Answer 1:

Security Question 2:

Security Answer 2:

Notes:

Website:

Username: Email:

Password:

Security Question 1:

Security Answer 1:

Security Question 2:

Security Answer 2:

Notes:

Website:

Username: Email:

Password:

Security Question 1:

Security Answer 1:

Security Question 2:

Security Answer 2:

Notes:

Website:

Username: Email:

Password:

Security Question 1:

Security Answer 1:

Security Question 2:

Security Answer 2:

Notes:

Website:

Username: ___________________ Email: ___________________

Password:

Security Question 1:

Security Answer 1:

Security Question 2:

Security Answer 2:

Notes:

Website:

Username: ___________________ Email: ___________________

Password:

Security Question 1:

Security Answer 1:

Security Question 2:

Security Answer 2:

Notes:

Website:

Username: ___________________ Email: ___________________

Password:

Security Question 1:

Security Answer 1:

Security Question 2:

Security Answer 2:

Notes:

Website:

Username: Email:

Password:

Security Question 1:

Security Answer 1:

Security Question 2:

Security Answer 2:

Notes:

Website:

Username: Email:

Password:

Security Question 1:

Security Answer 1:

Security Question 2:

Security Answer 2:

Notes:

Website:

Username: Email:

Password:

Security Question 1:

Security Answer 1:

Security Question 2:

Security Answer 2:

Notes:

Website:

Username: Email:

Password:

Security Question 1:

Security Answer 1:

Security Question 2:

Security Answer 2:

Notes:

Website:

Username: Email:

Password:

Security Question 1:

Security Answer 1:

Security Question 2:

Security Answer 2:

Notes:

Website:

Username: Email:

Password:

Security Question 1:

Security Answer 1:

Security Question 2:

Security Answer 2:

Notes:

Website:

Username: Email:

Password:

Security Question 1:

Security Answer 1:

Security Question 2:

Security Answer 2:

Notes:

Website:

Username: Email:

Password:

Security Question 1:

Security Answer 1:

Security Question 2:

Security Answer 2:

Notes:

Website:

Username: Email:

Password:

Security Question 1:

Security Answer 1:

Security Question 2:

Security Answer 2:

Notes:

Website:

Username: Email:

Password:

Security Question 1:

Security Answer 1:

Security Question 2:

Security Answer 2:

Notes:

Website:

Username: Email:

Password:

Security Question 1:

Security Answer 1:

Security Question 2:

Security Answer 2:

Notes:

Website:

Username: Email:

Password:

Security Question 1:

Security Answer 1:

Security Question 2:

Security Answer 2:

Notes:

Website:

Username: Email:

Password:

Security Question 1:

Security Answer 1:

Security Question 2:

Security Answer 2:

Notes:

Website:

Username: Email:

Password:

Security Question 1:

Security Answer 1:

Security Question 2:

Security Answer 2:

Notes:

Website:

Username: Email:

Password:

Security Question 1:

Security Answer 1:

Security Question 2:

Security Answer 2:

Notes:

Website:

Username: Email:

Password:

Security Question 1:

Security Answer 1:

Security Question 2:

Security Answer 2:

Notes:

Website:

Username: Email:

Password:

Security Question 1:

Security Answer 1:

Security Question 2:

Security Answer 2:

Notes:

Website:

Username: Email:

Password:

Security Question 1:

Security Answer 1:

Security Question 2:

Security Answer 2:

Notes:

Website:

Username: Email:

Password:

Security Question 1:

Security Answer 1:

Security Question 2:

Security Answer 2:

Notes:

Website:

Username: Email:

Password:

Security Question 1:

Security Answer 1:

Security Question 2:

Security Answer 2:

Notes:

Website:

Username: Email:

Password:

Security Question 1:

Security Answer 1:

Security Question 2:

Security Answer 2:

Notes:

Website:

Username: Email:

Password:

Security Question 1:

Security Answer 1:

Security Question 2:

Security Answer 2:

Notes:

Website:

Username: Email:

Password:

Security Question 1:

Security Answer 1:

Security Question 2:

Security Answer 2:

Notes:

Website:

Username: Email:

Password:

Security Question 1:

Security Answer 1:

Security Question 2:

Security Answer 2:

Notes:

Website:

Username: Email:

Password:

Security Question 1:

Security Answer 1:

Security Question 2:

Security Answer 2:

Notes:

Website:

Username: Email:

Password:

Security Question 1:

Security Answer 1:

Security Question 2:

Security Answer 2:

Notes:

Website:

Username: Email:

Password:

Security Question 1:

Security Answer 1:

Security Question 2:

Security Answer 2:

Notes:

Website:

Username: Email:

Password:

Security Question 1:

Security Answer 1:

Security Question 2:

Security Answer 2:

Notes:

Website:

Username: Email:

Password:

Security Question 1:

Security Answer 1:

Security Question 2:

Security Answer 2:

Notes:

Website:

Username: Email:

Password:

Security Question 1:

Security Answer 1:

Security Question 2:

Security Answer 2:

Notes:

Website:

Username: Email:

Password:

Security Question 1:

Security Answer 1:

Security Question 2:

Security Answer 2:

Notes:

Website:

Username: Email:

Password:

Security Question 1:

Security Answer 1:

Security Question 2:

Security Answer 2:

Notes:

Website:

Username: Email:

Password:

Security Question 1:

Security Answer 1:

Security Question 2:

Security Answer 2:

Notes:

Website:

Username: Email:

Password:

Security Question 1:

Security Answer 1:

Security Question 2:

Security Answer 2:

Notes:

Website:

Username: Email:

Password:

Security Question 1:

Security Answer 1:

Security Question 2:

Security Answer 2:

Notes:

Website:

Username: Email:

Password:

Security Question 1:

Security Answer 1:

Security Question 2:

Security Answer 2:

Notes:

Website:

Username: Email:

Password:

Security Question 1:

Security Answer 1:

Security Question 2:

Security Answer 2:

Notes:

Website:

Username: Email:

Password:

Security Question 1:

Security Answer 1:

Security Question 2:

Security Answer 2:

Notes:

Website:

Username: Email:

Password:

Security Question 1:

Security Answer 1:

Security Question 2:

Security Answer 2:

Notes:

Website:

Username: Email:

Password:

Security Question 1:

Security Answer 1:

Security Question 2:

Security Answer 2:

Notes:

Website:

Username: Email:

Password:

Security Question 1:

Security Answer 1:

Security Question 2:

Security Answer 2:

Notes:

Website:

Username: Email:

Password:

Security Question 1:

Security Answer 1:

Security Question 2:

Security Answer 2:

Notes:

Website:

Username: Email:

Password:

Security Question 1:

Security Answer 1:

Security Question 2:

Security Answer 2:

Notes:

Website:

Username: Email:

Password:

Security Question 1:

Security Answer 1:

Security Question 2:

Security Answer 2:

Notes:

Website:

Username: Email:

Password:

Security Question 1:

Security Answer 1:

Security Question 2:

Security Answer 2:

Notes:

Website:

Username: Email:

Password:

Security Question 1:

Security Answer 1:

Security Question 2:

Security Answer 2:

Notes:

Website:

Username: Email:

Password:

Security Question 1:

Security Answer 1:

Security Question 2:

Security Answer 2:

Notes:

Website:

Username: Email:

Password:

Security Question 1:

Security Answer 1:

Security Question 2:

Security Answer 2:

Notes:

Website:

Username: Email:

Password:

Security Question 1:

Security Answer 1:

Security Question 2:

Security Answer 2:

Notes:

Website:

Username: Email:

Password:

Security Question 1:

Security Answer 1:

Security Question 2:

Security Answer 2:

Notes:

Website:

Username: Email:

Password:

Security Question 1:

Security Answer 1:

Security Question 2:

Security Answer 2:

Notes:

Website:

Username: Email:

Password:

Security Question 1:

Security Answer 1:

Security Question 2:

Security Answer 2:

Notes:

Website:

Username: Email:

Password:

Security Question 1:

Security Answer 1:

Security Question 2:

Security Answer 2:

Notes:

Website:

Username: Email:

Password:

Security Question 1:

Security Answer 1:

Security Question 2:

Security Answer 2:

Notes:

Website:

Username: Email:

Password:

Security Question 1:

Security Answer 1:

Security Question 2:

Security Answer 2:

Notes:

Website:

Username: Email:

Password:

Security Question 1:

Security Answer 1:

Security Question 2:

Security Answer 2:

Notes:

Website:

Username: Email:

Password:

Security Question 1:

Security Answer 1:

Security Question 2:

Security Answer 2:

Notes:

Website:

Username: Email:

Password:

Security Question 1:

Security Answer 1:

Security Question 2:

Security Answer 2:

Notes:

Website:

Username: Email:

Password:

Security Question 1:

Security Answer 1:

Security Question 2:

Security Answer 2:

Notes:

Website:

Username: Email:

Password:

Security Question 1:

Security Answer 1:

Security Question 2:

Security Answer 2:

Notes:

Website:

Username: Email:

Password:

Security Question 1:

Security Answer 1:

Security Question 2:

Security Answer 2:

Notes:

Website:

Username: Email:

Password:

Security Question 1:

Security Answer 1:

Security Question 2:

Security Answer 2:

Notes:

Website:

Username: Email:

Password:

Security Question 1:

Security Answer 1:

Security Question 2:

Security Answer 2:

Notes:

Website:

Username: '   Email:

Password:

Security Question 1:

Security Answer 1:

Security Question 2:

Security Answer 2:

Notes:

Website:

Username: Email:

Password:

Security Question 1:

Security Answer 1:

Security Question 2:

Security Answer 2:

Notes:

Website:

Username: Email:

Password:

Security Question 1:

Security Answer 1:

Security Question 2:

Security Answer 2:

Notes:

Website:

Username: Email:

Password:

Security Question 1:

Security Answer 1:

Security Question 2:

Security Answer 2:

Notes:

Website:

Username: Email:

Password:

Security Question 1:

Security Answer 1:

Security Question 2:

Security Answer 2:

Notes:

Website:

Username: Email:

Password:

Security Question 1:

Security Answer 1:

Security Question 2:

Security Answer 2:

Notes:

Website:

Username: Email:

Password:

Security Question 1:

Security Answer 1:

Security Question 2:

Security Answer 2:

Notes:

Website:

Username: Email:

Password:

Security Question 1:

Security Answer 1:

Security Question 2:

Security Answer 2:

Notes:

Website:

Username: Email:

Password:

Security Question 1:

Security Answer 1:

Security Question 2:

Security Answer 2:

Notes:

Website:

Username: Email:

Password:

Security Question 1:

Security Answer 1:

Security Question 2:

Security Answer 2:

Notes:

Website:

Username: Email:

Password:

Security Question 1:

Security Answer 1:

Security Question 2:

Security Answer 2:

Notes:

Website:

Username: Email:

Password:

Security Question 1:

Security Answer 1:

Security Question 2:

Security Answer 2:

Notes:

Z

Website:

Username: Email:

Password:

Security Question 1:

Security Answer 1:

Security Question 2:

Security Answer 2:

Notes:

Website:

Username: Email:

Password:

Security Question 1:

Security Answer 1:

Security Question 2:

Security Answer 2:

Notes:

Website:

Username: Email:

Password:

Security Question 1:

Security Answer 1:

Security Question 2:

Security Answer 2:

Notes:

Website:

Username: Email:

Password:

Security Question 1:

Security Answer 1:

Security Question 2:

Security Answer 2:

Notes:

Website:

Username: Email:

Password:

Security Question 1:

Security Answer 1:

Security Question 2:

Security Answer 2:

Notes:

Website:

Username: Email:

Password:

Security Question 1:

Security Answer 1:

Security Question 2:

Security Answer 2:

Notes:

Z

Website:

Username: Email:

Password:

Security Question 1:

Security Answer 1:

Security Question 2:

Security Answer 2:

Notes:

Website:

Username: Email:

Password:

Security Question 1:

Security Answer 1:

Security Question 2:

Security Answer 2:

Notes:

Website:

Username: Email:

Password:

Security Question 1:

Security Answer 1:

Security Question 2:

Security Answer 2:

Notes:

Website:

Username: Email:

Password:

Security Question 1:

Security Answer 1:

Security Question 2:

Security Answer 2:

Notes:

Website:

Username: Email:

Password:

Security Question 1:

Security Answer 1:

Security Question 2:

Security Answer 2:

Notes:

Website:

Username: Email:

Password:

Security Question 1:

Security Answer 1:

Security Question 2:

Security Answer 2:

Notes:

Z

Website:

Username: Email:

Password:

Security Question 1:

Security Answer 1:

Security Question 2:

Security Answer 2:

Notes:

Website:

Username: Email:

Password:

Security Question 1:

Security Answer 1:

Security Question 2:

Security Answer 2:

Notes:

Website:

Username: Email:

Password:

Security Question 1:

Security Answer 1:

Security Question 2:

Security Answer 2:

Notes:

Website:

Username: Email:

Password:

Security Question 1:

Security Answer 1:

Security Question 2:

Security Answer 2:

Notes:

Website:

Username: Email:

Password:

Security Question 1:

Security Answer 1:

Security Question 2:

Security Answer 2:

Notes:

Website:

Username: Email:

Password:

Security Question 1:

Security Answer 1:

Security Question 2:

Security Answer 2:

Notes: